MW00745504

Essential Question
What can animals in stories teach us?

The Cat
and the Mice

by Ann Weil

illustrated by Roberta Collier-Morales

Cat liked mice.
He liked to **chase** mice.
He liked to **snatch** mice.

Then he liked to eat them.

The mice had a **meeting**.
"What can we do about
Cat?" they asked.

4

"We can make a **trap**!"

"I know," said the old mouse.
"Put a bell on the cat."

"Yes!" said the mice.
"Then we can hear the cat."

"We could run and hide,"
they said.

The mice were thrilled!

They had **solved**
the **problem**!

"But who will put the bell
on the cat?" asked a mouse.

The mice looked at the
old mouse.

"I can't do it," he said.
"I am too old!"

No mouse wanted to do it.

Fables teach us a **lesson**.
This fable's lesson is
"Easier said than done."

Respond to Reading

Summarize

Tell what the story was about. Use the chart to help you.

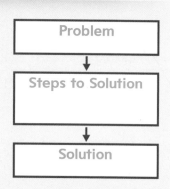

Problem

↓

Steps to Solution

↓

Solution

Text Evidence

1. What is the problem in the story? Problem and Solution

2. Reread page 9. Why are the mice *thrilled*? What is another word for *thrilled*? Vocabulary

3. Write about how the mice try to solve their problem. Write About Reading

Compare Texts
Read another animal story
that can teach a lesson.

Beware of Tiger!

There was a tiger.
It ate other animals.
That's what tigers do.
"If we heard it,
we could run away,"
said Deer.

"I have an idea," said
Pig. "Tie a rattle around
Tiger's neck!"

Deer agreed. He made the
rattle. He found a vine. He
gave these to Pig. "Put it
on Tiger," said Deer.

"No!" said Pig. "He will eat me!" Something moved behind them. Pig and deer ran away!

The lesson is: It is one thing to have an idea, and another to carry it out.

Make Connections

What did the animals in this story teach you? Essential Question

How are Pig and Deer like the mice? Text to Text

Focus on
Literary Elements

Dialogue Dialogue is what the characters in a story say.

What to Look for Look for quotation marks. They show where dialogue begins and ends. Here is an example:

"No!" said Pig.

Your Turn

Write two sentences of dialogue for an animal story. Use quotation marks around the words your characters say.